Stock Market Investing for Beginners:

10 Great Ways to Learn Trading Psychology Revealed by a Wall Street Insider, To Reach Your Financial Freedom

Table of Contents

Introduction

Chapter 1: Fundamental Valuation

Chapter 2: CAN SLIM

Chapter 3: Dogs of the Dow

Chapter 4: Value Investing

Chapter 5: Growth Investing

Chapter 6: Price Action Trading

Chapter 7: Reading the Charts

Chapter 8: Swing Trading

Chapter 9: Consolidation Patterns

Chapter 10: Momentum Trading

Conclusion

© Copyright 2018 by Dan Kirkmann - All rights reserved.

The follow eBook is reproduced below with the goal of providing information that is as accurate and reliable as possible. Regardless, purchasing this eBook can be seen as consent to the fact that both the publisher and the author of this book are in no way experts on the topics discussed within and that any recommendations or suggestions that are made herein are for entertainment purposes only. Professionals should be consulted as needed prior to undertaking any of the action endorsed herein.

This declaration is deemed fair and valid by both the American Bar Association and the Committee of Publishers Association and is legally binding throughout the United States.

Furthermore, the transmission, duplication or reproduction of any of the following work including specific information will be considered an illegal act irrespective of if it is done electronically or in print. This extends to creating a secondary or tertiary copy of the work or a recorded copy and is only allowed with express written consent from the Publisher. All additional right reserved.

The information in the following pages is broadly considered to be a truthful and accurate account of facts and as such any inattention, use or misuse of the information in question by the reader will render any resulting actions solely under their purview. There are no scenarios in which the publisher or the original author of this work can be in any fashion deemed liable for any hardship or damages that may befall them after undertaking information described herein.

Additionally, the information in the following pages is intended only for informational purposes and should thus be thought of as universal. As befitting its nature, it is presented without assurance regarding its prolonged validity or interim quality. Trademarks that are mentioned are done without written consent and can in no way be considered an endorsement from the trademark holder.

Introduction

Congratulations on downloading *Stock Market Investing for Beginners: 10 Great Ways to Learn Trading Psychology Revealed by a Wall Street Insider, To Reach Your Financial Freedom* and thank you for doing so. Trading on the stock market can be an exhilarating, infuriating and, above all, profitable experience, but only if you have the strategies in place to ensure that you aren't simply throwing money at the wall and seeing what sticks.

Unfortunately, there are a lot of strategies out there, and many of them don't work as advertised, and of those that do work many aren't designed for beginners which can make it difficult for you to get started successfully. Luckily for you, I have been trading in the stock market successfully for more than 10 years, and day trading as my primary source of income for more than half that time which means you can learn from my mistakes and focus on the types of successful strategies that any trader can put to use with a little practice.

In the following chapters, you will find strategies that focus both on fundamental and technical analysis as well as both short and long timeframes to ensure that there is something for you no matter what your trading preferences and inclinations. Don't forget, the best way to learn a new strategy is to practice with real money as opposed to a demo account. This way you can get the mentality of the strategy down, not just the motions of it. Give each a fair shot and you should be able to find at least a few that strike your fancy. Good luck!

There are plenty of books on this subject on the market, thanks again for choosing this one! Every effort was made to ensure it is full of as much useful information as possible, please enjoy!

Chapter 1: Fundamental Valuation

While the phrase fundamental valuation may sound exceedingly complex, the process is actually quite straightforward. As long as you are ready to put in the time and do the research, there is no reason you shouldn't be able to look at a company's fundamentals and determine what it is actually worth as opposed to what the market believes it is worth at the moment. While there are numerous different ways of determining the intrinsic value of a company, they are all ultimately going to get you to the same point, which is being able to accurately determine if a company is currently worth what all its discounted cash flow says it is.

While this might not be the most obvious means of determining value, the fundamentals at play make sense when you consider the way in which a business generates value for its stock holders. After all, a company is only worth what you can take out of it after all its expenses have all been factored in. Essentially the basis of intrinsic value is profits which are just expenses subtracted from revenue.

Fool theory: One important assumption to be aware of when using this theory is that investors are rational which means that no one is going to pay more for a business that what its discounted cash flow says it is worth. Due to the fact that buying a stock is akin to buying ownership in the company, this assumption applies to the stock market as well. If this is the case, then you might be asking yourself why it is that stocks fluctuate in value so much when the value of the underlying company is unlikely to change at anywhere near the same level is the fact that most traders are viewing their stocks the wrong way in the first place and instead simply view them as vehicles for trading. As such, the value of the cash flow is incorrectly discounted as long as they can still make a profit on the sale.

Cynical professional traders have dubbed this the greater fool theory as the profit that is earned on the trade isn't based on anything tangible, like the value of the company, but is instead based solely around the speculation that you can always sell it to another investor (the titular fool). Meanwhile, speculative traders like to argue that fundamental investors are leaving themselves open to the market by failing to take into account various market trends and tendencies.

This never ending debate illustrates the difference between the fundamental investor and the technical investor, and this book offers plenty of strategies that cater to each. An investor who focuses primarily on technical trading is not going to be interested in intrinsic value and will instead focus on the trends the market is currently experiencing as it is expressed in their favored charts.

While the idea of discounting cash flow might make sense in theory, it can be a little bit more complicated to implement in real life, at least at first. Specifically, one of the biggest challenges that you will face is going to be deciding how far into the future you are going to want to forecast the case flow of the company in question. This is because it can be difficult to predict the potential profits for a company for a single year, much less five or 10. In fact, a majority of companies out there could experience a scenario where they were out of business in five years; on the contrary, they could also stumble into an idea that ensures they are going to be around for the next 100 years instead. This general level of uncertainty explains why there are so many different models when it comes to discounting the cash flow.

The biggest problem when it comes to projecting future profits comes from accounting for the different rate that the company is sure to grow at in the given timeframe. To avoid this problem you are going to need to do two things, first, you will need to determine the sum of the discounted cash flow for each of the next five years. Second, you will need to determine the residual value which can be done by taking the sum of the future cash flows starting with the sixth year.

As an example, if you take a company with an anticipated growth rate (for the next five years) at a rate of 15 percent each year, before slowing to a steady five percent per year, then you would need to add together the initial cash flows once they have been discounted to the current year. This will then allow you to easily determine the present value which will allow you to look to the second stage of the process and consider the cash flow pat the first five years while taking into account the expected growth rate of five percent. Of course, the cash flow for these subsequent years is then going to be discounted back to the fifth year before being added together before being discounted back to the current year. With that done you will then want to combine the total and the price value as determined by the first five years.

This results will then make it possible for you to determine an estimate of the intrinsic value of the company you are considering buying stock in. If this estimate ultimately ends up being greater than the company's current market capitalization rate then you can buy with relative confidence. Don't forget, the market capitalization can be thought of as the total value of the company currently based on the sum total of all of the available stock for the company that is currently on the market.

Qualitative factors: It is also important to take a look at the qualitative aspects of the company in general in order to determine if they are going to be a truly reliable investment. To do so, the first thing you will want to do is to look to the business model that the company is currently working with. A business model is essentially just a simplified explanation of what exactly the company does. You can generally find a company business model on the company's website, though it might still be quite complicated, even if from the outside what the company does is fairly straight forward.

While this might not seem necessary for all companies, it is an easy thing to check and you may well be glad you did. The best example of this occurred in the 90s with a company called Boston Chicken. Now, based on the name, you would be forgiven for assuming that this company sold chicken or at least chicken-like products. In reality, however, their business model relied on selling franchises with extremely high fees to individual business owners. Now this stock was on fire for most of 1992, burning up the charts and being seen by virtually everyone as an auto-buy. However, once the market got a better idea of what was actually going on, and the fact that the franchises that were sold were not turning a profit, the company, and its stock price, collapsed, taking plenty of traders' money with it.

While this is not to say that you need to understand all the minutiae that make up the company's day to day, it is important to grasp the fundamentals to ensured you don't end up in Boston Chicken scenario. Doing so will ensure that you are able to accurately determine the true drivers for future growth for the company without leaving yourself open to the potential to be blindsided later on.

Competitive advantage: When it comes to deciding if a company is worth pursuing is the odds that the company can properly retain an advantage against its competition. A reliable competitive advantage is something like Microsoft's functional monopoly in the PC space or the brand clout that comes along with Pepsi. Advantages like these essentially create a moat around that section of the market that make it difficult for anyone to ever come in and breach their market share. If you can find few companies like this to invest in when they are young then you could potentially expect quality dividends for decades to come.

Competitive advantage materializes in two ways, competitive advantage or operational effectiveness, essentially either doing something different or doing the same thing better than everyone else. Competitive advantage occurs when a company outperforms its rivals by doing something different, or possibly by performing nearly the same service in a markedly different way. Operational effectiveness, on the other hand, occurs when the company is better at doing the same thing everyone in the niche is doing as well.

Generally speaking, competitive advantage can stick around in the long-term if a company positions itself in a competitive position that is unique, or when its activities are uniquely tailored to the strategy in question. On the other hand, it may come with well-defined tradeoffs or choices when compared to the competition (think Apple and Microsoft). The other alternative is that it has a higher degree of fit across a wide variety of activities in such a way that make its activity systems and parts sustainable in the long-term. Finally, the operational effectiveness could simply just be on point to such a degree that no one can touch them in that regard.

Chapter 2: CAN SLIM

The CAN SLIM strategy is a great way for new traders to get used to screening the market to help themselves always make the best available choice. What makes this strategy particularly effective is that it focuses specifically on a powerful mix of tangible specifics like earnings, as well as a variety of intangibles that help to set the best companies apart from the rest. There is evidence that it works as well as there have been plenty of big name companies that previously went through a phase that would have made them great choices via the CAN SLIM process.

Earnings from the most recent corner: The first thing you will need to keep an eye out for when using the CAN SLIM system is the most recent earnings that are available for the company in question. You will need these earning to show a dramatic increase when compared to where they were 12 months prior. The smallest amount of growth that you are going to want to consider moving forward with is going to be 18 percent.

This cutoff limit has traditionally been enough to show increasing growth continually, for the near future as for the 50 years between 1950 and 2000 more than 70 percent of the companies that met this standard went on to see significant growth in the coming quarters. If you are interested in only sticking with the best of the best then you are going to want to stick to companies that saw a 50 percent increase in profits over the past year.

In order to ensure that you are determining your earnings as accurately as possible, don't forget to take the time to find the difference between the figures you are looking at are of a quality that they will be useful as opposed to only showing what the company wants the public to see. This means you are going to want to go beyond what is available from the most recent shareholders meeting to looking for any disparities between truth and fiction as they could end up saving you serious cash in the long run.

Annual earnings: While year over year quarterly improvement is a good place to start, it is also crucial that you look for stocks that are connected to companies that have seen their growth increase at a steady rate for at least five years straight. During this same time, you are going to want to keep an eye out for companies that have seen 25 percent growth per year, though 50 percent is the number you should always be on the lookout for.

Changes to the company: In order to properly narrow down your search, you will typically find the most reliable results when it comes to companies that have recently seen major changes to their corporate structure as it is these types of changes that are likely to ultimately precede events that are more likely to see the company jump to the next level. The specifics of what happened in this instance are nearly as important as the fact that, statistically speaking, 95 percent of companies that experience this type of growth started with a significant change to the status quo.

Supply and demand: It is often easier for smaller companies that have fewer shares of stock on the market to see major gains in a shorter amount of time. What's more, most of the time the companies that see the largest gains are those that have fewer than 25 million shares outstanding. The reason that this is the case is that, when compared to a larger company, it takes much less demand for the smaller company to see far greater gains.

This is due to the fact that the moves the larger company makes tend to be large enough that they are seen and judged right away, causing their stock price to typically decrease until people understand what it is they want. When compared to major players, whose investments are typically large enough to affect share price directly, smaller, private investors have an advantage in that they can buy into, or get out of, smaller companies without moving the price too much if things don't go according to plan.

Leader: THE CAN SLIM method also work by making a swift distinction between those who are likely to blaze a trail and those that are far more likely to play catchup instead. After all, it is only natural that industries have companies that continually buck trends, just as it will have those that are always late to the party, regardless of what the next big thing might be. As the first type of companies are always better off than the second, it is important that you can tell the laggards from the leaders.

The best place to start is by determining the relative strength of the company in question compared to its market. The most efficient means of doing so is going to be looking to the rate of change several of the companies in the industry have experienced for the past year before dividing that amount by the rate of change that the related index saw over the same period. The rate of change the stock experiences can then be divided y the benchmark rate of change in order to properly determine the overall relative strength value. The most effective way of choosing which stocks to focus on is by focusing on those that are within the top 20 or 10 percent of your favored index.

Institutional support: If you aren't quite sure that you are making the right choice on a given stock, a great way to double check your results is to look at the amount of institutional sponsorship the company currently has. Institutional sponsorship is another name for buy-in from professional traders so if you see that you are following the major players in the market then you can safely assume you are on the right track.

While a certain level of institutional interest will show that you are on the right track, it is important to use the overall level of institutional interest as a means of determining whether the ship has sailed on this particular stock. Generally speaking, if the stock in question is already owned by a majority of professional traders, then you can safely assume that the ship has sailed on this particular stock and that you would be better served looking elsewhere first. This is the case as a company with too much institutional ownership runs the risk of a substantial sell-off should the slightest hint of bad news develop which means that it wouldn't take much to send the stock price plummeting.

Direction of the market: In order to ensure that you are picking the right stocks a majority of the time, it is important that you always make the time you need to consider the overall market sentiment to ensure you aren't going against the current trend without realizing it. The best way of making sure that this is not the case is to keep an eye on the market by watching its overall daily movement and volume.

Chapter 3: Dogs of the Dow

The Dogs of the Dow strategy is as simple as it is effective, all you need to do is to pick one of the top 10 companies that are currently at the top of the Dow Jones Industrial Average when taking overall dividend yield into account. The Dow Jones Industrial Average (DJIA) is a price-weighted average of the 30 most significant stocks currently being traded on the New York Stock Exchange. THE DJIA is home to many of the largest companies in the world including the likes of Exxon Mobil and Disney. General Electric, the last company to have been a member of the DJIA since its inception was dropped from the index in June of 2018.

The DJIA is a metric of the current strength of the US economy overall. When it was first created near the turn of the last century it primarily focused on industrial companies but it has since steadily changed with the times in order to stay abreast of the width and breadth of the American economy. The index is price weighted so that those stocks with a higher share price count towards the overall value more than those with a lower share price do.

The Dogs of the Dow strategy then is exceedingly simple, and it is a great way to put your money into the stock market while at the same time virtually guaranteeing a reliable return indefinitely. To get started, all you will need to do is allocate your available trading capital into a mix of three of the top 10 companies on the list, before then holding on to the index and shuffling around the specifics as needed. Generally speaking, you will then want to change out a few of your choices each year, based on those that seem as though they are going to return the highest dividend, you will then pick up a few of the stocks lower on the list and wait for them to improve. Rinse and repeat.

At the end of the year you will then want to reassess the current state of the DJIA and look for the companies that have the greatest dividend yield, before equally weighting out each of them in your portfolio so that it remains as balanced as possible. While this is a very long-term strategy, you can count on it to reliably return positive results year in and year out indefinitely as long as you play your cards right.

DJIA companies have a long history of remaining extremely stable, regardless of what the stock market as a whole might be doing as the size of the companies in question means that they can handle down years better than most, regardless of the severity of the issues in question. What's more, inclusion in the DJIA is gated by a committee which means the companies you have to choose from have already been hand selected because they are the best of the best.

Historically speaking this strategy has done about as well as can be expected, between 1957 and 2003, the companies recommended by this strategy outperformed the Dow overall by an average of 3 percent. This, in turn, leads to a return rate of 14.3 percent in the same timeframe as opposed to just 11 percent when viewing the Dow as a whole. Between 1973 and 1996, this return was even higher, and the Dogs averaged 20.3 percent annually compared to the Dow's 15.8 percent.

Dogs of the Dow variations: As the Dogs of the Dow strategy is exceedingly simple, there have been many attempts to improve on it over the years, some far more successful than others. One of the most effective is known as the Dow 5 which encourages users to buy into the five lowest stocks on the Dogs of the Dow list and then invest equally in each. The Dow 4, meanwhile, takes the top four of the Dow 5 and invests equally in each. Meanwhile, the Foolish 4 uses the Dow 4 stocks but recommends putting 20 percent into the top three of these and then the remaining 40 percent into the one at the bottom of the pile.

While it may seem as those these additional strategies are all just looking for ways to complicate a good thing, the reasoning behind it all is solid, and the results it has seen over the years should speak for themselves. After all, while these strategies focus on the bottom stocks in the Dogs, this still represents many of the top companies in the country, if not the world. For example, at the time of this writing, those that would qualify for the alternate Dogs of the Dow strategies include Proctor and Gamble, McDonald's and Coca-Cola. The plan with each is then to hold as long as possible, making a profit from the dividends until the price jumped to such a point that not selling would be a poor choice.

Chapter 4: Value Investing

Value investing is one of the most effective and well-known means of picking stocks and has been ever since it was developed by a pair of professors out of Colombia University in the 1930s. While it is quite easy to understand, be prepared to put in some practice before you can use it easily on the open market. To start, all you will need to do is to find a company that is currently worth more than what its current stock price indicates.

When you find a company whose value compared to its fundamentals is where you want it to be, you are going to want to jump in as quickly as possible as the market is bound to correct itself sooner than later which means if you wait even a minute too long then you are going to find yourself having a difficult time making a profit

When it comes to value investing, the most important thing to keep in mind is that there is a difference between stocks that are currently undervalued for one reason or another and those stocks that are actually almost worthless. Fail to make the right distinction and you will end up buying into stocks that are only going to decrease in value. an example, if a company's stock was previously trading at about $25 per share and it suddenly drops to $10, this doesn't mean that you will automatically want to put it in the buy camp until you determine what caused the drop. This is because the drop could be a perfectly appropriate response by the market to an overall decrease in the company's value. To ensure the stock is the bargain it appears to be you would need to take a closer look at the fundamentals.

Legendary money maker Warren Buffet is perhaps the most successful proponent of this strategy of all time. In 1967 shares of Berkshire Hathaway were worth only $12 per share and he held them until 2002 when they were worth a staggering $70,900 per share. Now, these results are certainly the exception, not the rule, but they go to show just how powerful this form of investing can be if it is done correctly.

To ensure you get the most bang for your buck when it comes to value investing you are going to want to ensure that you focus on the types of stocks whose share price is no more than 66 percent of what your research indicates it should actually be worth. From there, you will also want to look for companies that have a P/E ratio that is less than 10 percent of its related equity. Furthermore, you will need to look for companies that have a P/E ratio to growth ratio is positive which can be accomplished by dividing the P/E ratio by the growth rate of the company's earnings, is less than 1.

Other important things to keep in mind is that you will always want the stock price to stay lower than the tangible book value as the type of company you are looking for is always going to have less debt than they do equity. The current assets of the company should then be about twice their overall liability and they should both have a dividend yield that is about 60 percent when compared to the yield estimates for its long-term bond. On top of all of that, the growth earnings for the company should be a minimum of seven percent every year for at least 10 years.

Don't forget to also factor in a bit of a safety net in terms of the margin, just in case things don't work out according to plan. This will ensure that you have the required breathing room should errors appear that were not visible when you calculated the company's intrinsic value. To factor in this margin of error, you will simply subtract 10 percent from the intrinsic value number that you calculated.

Chapter 5: Growth Investing

Much like the name implies, growth investing is all about looking at the future of a company as opposed to their current specifics. In fact, the current price of the stock of the company in question is barely a factor when everything is done properly. This strategy is all about buying into companies that are currently trading above their true intrinsic value based on the assumption that this value will eventually grow to a point that the valuation is lower than it should be.

In order to best take advantage of this strategy, the first thing you will want to do is ensure you are always on the lookout for younger companies as these are the ones that are most likely to grow rapidly in the reasonably near future, especially when compared to companies that are far more well-established. This strategy ultimately hinges on the assumption that a growth in earnings or revenue will directly translate into an increase in the underlying stock price one way or the other. Additional viable choices include companies whose industry is currently seeing lots of growth as well as those that are in fields related to new technological advancements.

From there, profits are realized not from the dividends of the stock but based on the capital gains they generate instead. Companies of this type will rarely generate any dividends at all as all the profits that they may generate are put right back into the company to fuel future expansion instead.

The simple fact that every company is different means that there are few true guidelines when it comes to properly finding growth companies. Nevertheless, there is a general framework that you can use to complete your analysis that should at least ensure you are on the right track. Some of what you will need to be aware of includes the current state of the company where compared to its past performance in addition to the performance when compared to its competition.

If the company is valued at 4 billion dollars or more then you will want to see at least 5 percent growth per year. If the company is worth at least 400 million dollars then you are going to want to look for a growth rate of 7 percent. If the company is currently worth less than 400 million dollars then you will want to see a minimum of 12 percent growth.

Beyond just the annual growth, you are also going to want to take into account the company's forward earning growth which needs to be at least 10 percent at the bare minimum, though 15 percent is likely a more reliable amount. You will also always want to be aware that these numbers are just predictions which means they are always subject to change. Finally, you are going to want to ensure that you only move forward with stocks that are likely to double within five years' time, if this doesn't seem like a realistic possibility, then what you are looking at isn't actually a growth stock. While this might seem like a stiff requirement, the fact of the matter is that a 10 percent growth rate will see a company hit a price doubling within seven years which means it is only a little bit faster than average.

Growth at a reasonable price: Growth at a reasonable price (GARP) investing is a combination of growth investing and value investing. In order to use it effectively, you will need to remain vigilant when it comes to finding companies that, while a little undervalued, still have the potential to see major growth in the long-term. The best case scenario here is to look for stocks that are less undervalued than what you would look for with value investing and slightly less impressive future potential than those you would follow with strict growth investing.

In much the same way that growth investing is, GARP investing is mostly concerned with the growth of the prospective company. This means that in order to use this method as effectively as possible you will need to keep a constant lookout for companies with high positive earnings from the past few years as well as positive earnings projections for the next few years as well. Unlike with pure growth investing, the best range of growth from these types of companies is going to be between 25 and 50 percent over the next five years, rather than the full 100 percent. GARP investing also works under the assumption that the higher the growth rate overall, the higher the amount of risk the investment will be as well.

Among other things, GARP investing is also known to shares some of the same metrics for determining potentially worthwhile trade by looking for companies that already have positive earnings momentum as well as a strong cash flow. As an added bonus you are going to have a great deal of additional freedom when it comes to choosing the best companies for you based on your subjective ideas as this is an important part of the GARP process as well. The specifics don't matter, what is most important is that you take the time to thoroughly analyze companies in relation to their specific contexts as there is no formal definition of what makes a good GARP investment.

Finally, you are going to want to keep a close lookout for P/E ratios that had already exceed those that are typically taken into account with value investing. While a growth investor needs a P/E ratio that is at least 50 times greater than earnings, GARP investors are going to be looking in the 15 to 25 range.

Chapter 6: Price Action Trading

While many active traders make use of a wide variety of complicated indicators, I've always found it especially useful to take advantage of price action trading during times when I don't have the ability or the desire to do a more in depth study of the market. At its most basic, price action is a way for traders to accurately pinpoint the current state of the market by determining how the prices are acting.

As such, if you are a trader that is interested in getting started as quickly as possible then sticking with price action trading, for now, can save you serous time as you only have to spend your time and focus studying the market as it is in the present. What' smore, focusing exclusively on the price and just the price will make it easier for you to block out some of the useless information that is constantly creating static in the market.

Getting started: In order to use price action to trade successfully, the first thing you will need should be included in your trading platform, regardless of which type you prefer, the price bar. A price par is a simple representation of the relevant price information for the stock in question over a specific period of time. In order to create the most accurate price bar possible, you will need four different pieces of information.

The first piece of price bar information you need is the amount the stock opened at, followed by the overall high for the day as well as the low and the close for the day as well. With those details in hand, the data is then plotted in such a way that it should create a box with a line through it. The two end points of the line represent the high and low, respectively, when the top and bottom edges of the box represented the opening and closing prices, respectively. Stocks that end up on an appreciation profit end up one color and those that end in a loss are given another color.

The result is then referred to as a candlestick and, in addition to summarizing the whole day's worth of information it also provides details that are crucial for ensuring the right price action trade decision is made when the time is right. These bonus details include things like the range of the stock, the body of the stock and the upper and lower wick.

Range: The range is the visual representation of the market's current level of volatility. The bigger the box is in relation to the line, alternately called the wick, the greater the amount of activity the market is currently experiences and the more volatility as well. The greater the amount of volatility the market is experiencing, the greater the amount of risk you take on when you make a move.

Body: The body refers to the actual, physical, orientation of the box in question, this means that if the close is above the open then this means the market improved and if the price closes below the open it means the market decreased in value. What's more, when it comes to looking at the box you will want to keep in mind how large the box is when compared to the wick. The larger the box is in relation to the wick, the greater the strength of the market overall. If there is no visible bar to speak of then the market is said to be undecided. If you come across traders talking about a marubozu, this is a candle with no wick and doji is a market that is still undecided.

Wicks: Once you have a clear grasp on the body as well as the range of a given candle, you will then be able to easily determine the information that the upper wick has to tell you. The upper wick determines the topmost price point for the stock for the timeframe you are watching before it was unable to match market movement and had the price drop off. What this wick says is that once the price reached the top point for the day the number of sellers outpaced the number of buyers so that the price dropped as opposed to rising.

What this means is that the top wick is essentially the amount of pressure the stock experienced in this period of time. In much the same way, the lower wick indicates the strength of the pressure to buy in the same timeframe. The longer the wick in either direction, the more pressure that was put on the stock in a given direction.

Secondary price bar: If you add an additional price bar to your existing analysis then you will find that you have created a pair of cornerstones that will make it easier for you to test the price while ensuring it has the proper context as well. Essentially, the second bar is going to provide a way to determine if the data from the first bar is actually relevant or merely an irrelevant outlier. Specifically, it is useful when it comes to things like determining if a bar that appears wide is actually just on par with the other bars from the same timeframe.

This, in turn, makes it possible for you to describe the price action in a more precise way than would otherwise be possible. What's more, having a second price bar will allow you to determine if the price level will then be enough to either break through the existing levels of resistance or support. If the second bar shows the same level of support or resistance, then it is unlikely the price action will remain strong enough in order to break through it. Furthermore, if the two candles both have differing levels of resistance or support it is far more likely that a quality breakthrough will be made.

Third price bar: Once you add in a third price bar you will be able to confirm your existing hypothesis that adding in the second bar allowed you to create. This third bar should then be shown to much in such a way that it either completely confirms or denies the expectations the market presented you with to that point. The idea here is that if a market is already strong then it will continue to be so, and if it is weak then it will continue to be weak. If the market lacks inertia, then it is possible for a change to materialize at virtually any time. It is thus important to ensure you keep in mind that even with three bars the results are still only going to apply to the short-term and taking this pattern to be anything other than short-term is going to be a huge risk assuming you don't follow up properly.

Chapter 7: Reading the Charts

In order to ensure that your successful trade percentage only improves with time, it is important to recognize the common patterns that will often show up time and again when using technical analysis. Technical analysis is a great choice for those that prefer to determine the likely performance of the future by looking to the past, without having to dig through piles of paperwork and data to do so. While the past can't predict the future with 100 percent certainty, it can get closer than you might think.

Price charts: A price chart is a crucial part of technical analysis, essentially just a chart with an x and a y axis when the price can be tracked across the vertical axis and the time can be tracked via the horizontal axis. While there are dozens of different charts to choose from, each with specific strengths and weaknesses, the ones you will want to focus on to start are the point and click chart, the bar chart, the line chart and the candlestick chart discussed in a previous chapter.

Line chart: The simplest of all the charts, the line chart only shows the closing price for a specific stock for a certain period of time. The lines are formed from a grouping of closing prices as determined by the market that is then connected in an effort to determine what, if any, trends might currently be in play. You won't be able to find any additional details from this chart, but that can still be a positive as it makes it easy to determine the types of trends you are looking for without having to worry about any noise in the chart getting in the way.

Bar chart: The bar chart adds additional details to the line chart by providing an overall greater degree of detail in regard to the specifics of the day. The top and bottom bars represent the high and low for the day while the price at closing is shown on the right side of the bar as a dash. The left-side dash then shows the starting price and if the stock increased in value then the bar will be shaded black, while it will instead be either clear or red if the price dropped by close.

Point and figure chart: While not seen as frequently as some of the other charts, the point and figure chart was created more than a hundred years ago and it is still useful today. This chart accurately reflects price movement, just not volume or timing which means it is purely a price indicator which means it can be read clearly as it doesn't worry about any related market noise.

A point and figure chart can be clearly picked out from the other types of charts as it is comprised of Xs and Os rather than lines and points. The Xs will indicate points where positive trends occurred while the Os will indicate periods of downward movement. The chart will then have a list of number and letters listed along the bottom of the chart that corresponds to specific dates. This type of chart will then make it clear the amount the price will need to move to turn an X into an O and vice versa.

Trend and range: In order to ensure you can use technical analysis properly, it is important to decide early on if you are more likely to trade based on trend or trade based on range. While they are both going to still be related to price, the concepts are quite different from one another and favoring one means ignoring the other. If you are interested in trading via trend then this means you want to go with the flow and trade whatever stocks the majority is trading.

If this is the case, then your goal would be to determine the trends that are likely to be appearing in the near future to ensure that you have as much time as possible to take full advantage of the situation. If you want to move forward with this type of trading then you will want to stick to smaller trades as the trades you do make are likely to be riskier than would otherwise be the case as a trend might fail to appear as anticipated at any time. If you like the idea of high risk and high reward then trading based on trend is for you.

If you are looking for something that is somewhat safer, then you will likely wan to go with range trading instead. When trading via range, you are looking for stocks that can be predicted with almost 100 percent certainty so that you know when the positive or negative movement is coming ahead of time and can plan accordingly. You don't need to worry about finding the best entry point possible, or the like, you will simply need to ensure that you can get in on the ground floor for the next time the cycle is going to repeat itself. Range trading can take more time to get working properly, however, so it is best to have a larger bankroll when aiming to successfully put it into effect.

Chapter 8: Swing Trading

Generally speaking, swing trading is somewhere between day trading an not quite as long as investment trading as positions taken rarely last more than two week, and even then only when the trend they are based on is extremely strong. With swing trading, the goal is to identify the overall trend the stock is likely to take and then capture gains within that trend.

Technical analysis is a natural fit here as a means by which traders can take advantage of the trend by ensuring their trades are as effective as possible. Swing trading is often riskier than investment trading and also includes higher commission costs as well. Successful swing traders tend to work the main trend that a chart is presenting at any given time. There are also swing trading opportunities that manifest when a specific stock begins moving back and forth between support and resistance points and swing traders will take long positions when the price reaches the support level and short positions when it nears the resistance level.

Bullish trades: Due to the fact that stock market prices rarely move in a straight line, bullish swing traders typically need to look for initial upward movement as the primary part of a trend before expecting a reversal, otherwise known as a counter trend. Once this counter trend has successfully completed its arc, there should then be a resumption of upward movement. Due to the fact that it is difficult to determine the length of the primary counter trend then you will wan to enter into a bullish swing trade only once the counter trend has ended and the uptrend has restarted.

With this out of the way, you should then be able to determine the ideal time to enter a specific trade by isolating the relevant movement of the counter trend. A good way to do this is by determining when the stock trades at a price that is higher than the previous high. The entry point that you should find will then most likely be comparable to the price point from the previous few days as well in order to accurately determine risk as well as the potential upside for your target.

To do so, you will need to begin by locating the lowest point that the counter trend produced which should be considered the stop out point. This means that if the price drops below this point at any time then you will want to exit the trade to ensure you limit your possibility for potential losses. With this out of the way, you will then want to seek out the highest possible point associated with the uptrend before it becomes a counter trend as this will be a target for profits. As such, if the price rises past this point then you will want to exit with half of your holdings before setting a new price target of the rest to ensure you are able to take advantage of the stronger than anticipated trend for as long as possible.

The difference between the two points will mark the amount you can expect to realistically make on the trade, while the difference between the entry and exit points will determine your overall risk. If you are just starting a swing trade then you will want to ensure that you are trading into a scenario where you have at least twice the chance to profit compared to what it is you are putting at risk.

After you have determined that the trade is worth the risk, the next step will be to enter a buy-stop limit order to ensure that the moment the stock hits your desired entry point the order will activate and execute. After the option is open, you will then want to enter a one-cancels-other order to sell the stock as soon as it hits either the stop-loss price or the price where you are happy taking your profits and running. Thus, as soon as one gets the go ahead the other will be automatically canceled.

Bearish entry points: While rarely as easy to predict as uptrends, downtrends tend to follow all the same patterns just in reverse. They will likely move in a downward pattern, hit a point of retracement, reverse and repeat. After this has happened several times, it will then be far easier to see. Throughout all of this time, it should be possible to see the bearish retracement and rallies forming as a counter trend.

Tactics that are useful when dealing with a positive trend will typically work with a negative trend as well. You will also still only want to enter into a bearish swing trade after it is clear that the downward movement is actually the trend and not the byproduct of a retracement that you didn't see previously. In order to properly ensure that this will remain the case, you will need to pay close attention and wait for the point where the stock decreases to a point that is lower than the lowest point of the counter trend.

When dealing with a bearish swing trade, the stop out point is going to be the highest point that can be found in relation to the latest counter trend. The entry point would then be compared to the stop out along with the target point which will make it fairly straight forward when it comes to determining the risks and rewards that are in play. The profit target is going to be the point of the lowest price from the overall downtrend.

Chapter 9: Consolidation Patterns

Consolidation is the term used in technical analysis as a means to describe the fact that the price of a given stock tends to stick to the same pattern, regardless of the trading level that you view it from. More practically speaking, consolidation can be thought of as the period of indecisiveness that is guaranteed to come to an end after the price moves outside the existing pattern. These types of consolidation are surprisingly common and can be found across any price chart at nearly any timeframe.

When they do appear, technical traders tend to use them as a means of finding levels of resistance and support so that they can ensure the buying and selling decisions they make are as informed as possible. These levels are generated by the underlying asset and the fact that it is likely to vary a predetermined amount over a given period of time. This means that once the price moves outside either the pre-existing resistance or support level, volatility will increase dramatically as a result.

This volatile period is when smart traders will jump in to make serious profits in a short period of time. Furthermore, many technical traders believe that the breakout does occur on the side of the resistance then the price is going to typically continue to move upward which means you would want to go long in response. However, if the breakout instead occurs so that it is on par with the existing support then it is likely that the price is going to continue to decrease which means you will want to take a short position instead.

Flags and pennants: Both pennants and flags are signs of retracements or deviations from the existing trend that eventually become visible in the short tern if viewed in comparison to the existing trend. Retracements rarely lead to breakouts occurring in either direction, but the underlying asset likely won't be following the dominant trend in the first place so this shouldn't be much of an issue. However, the absence of a breakout will still result in a shorter trend overall. The resistance and support lines of the pennant occur within a much larger overall trend before coming together in a point. A flag is quite similar with the exception that its support and resistance lines come together in a parallel fashion instead.

Pennants and flags are both more likely to be visible within the middle portion of the primary trend. They also tend to last around two weeks on average before merging once again with the primary trend line. They are frequently associated with falling volume which means that if you see a flag or pennant with volume that isn't dropping then what you are likely really seeing is a reversal.

Head and Shoulders: If you are looking for indicators of the length of a particular trend then the head and shoulders formation of three peaks within the price chart tends to indicate an overall bearish pattern moving forward. The peaks to either side of the main peak should generally be a little small than the main peak which makes up the head. The price is the neckline in this scenario and when it reaches the right shoulder you can generally expect the price to drop off steeply.

This formation most frequently occurs when a large group of traders ends up holding out for a final price increase after a long run of gains has already dropped most traders out of the running. If this occurs and the trend changes, then the price will fall and the head and shoulders will become visible. It is also possible for the opposite to appear in the form of a reverse head and shoulders. If you see this pattern then you can expect the price to soon be on the rise.

Cup and handle: This formation typically appears when the stock in question reaches a peak and then falls off it sharply for the majority of the trading period or possibly longer. The security will then rebound after a certain point which means it will be time to buy. This indicator typically shows that a given trend is on the rise so you will want to take advantage of it while you can.

The handle often forms on the cup when those who bought in at a previous high get tired of waiting for the best possible price and decide to sell which, in turn, provides new investors a viable entry point. This type of formation is often slow to form and can even take up to a year to form in some instances. The ideal time to jump on this trend is when the handle has just started to form. If you can see the cup but no handle then you are going to want to watch the daily patterns form to help you determine when the handle is likely to make an appearance.

Chapter 10: Momentum Trading

Taking advantage of momentum trading is a great way to boost your profits and it can be extremely effective almost as soon as you start as long as you use it properly. The goal with this strategy is to choose trades that have already proven to show strong signs of momentum so that you can exploit this fact as much as possible. What's even better, all you really need to use this strategy successfully is the ability to take note of the degree to which a specific stock is moving, something that you are going to be doing anyway.

Momentum can be thought of as the rate at which a stock is accelerating either the rate at it moves or even the strength with which it is moving in a specific direction. When it comes to making the most of this strategy you will always want to start with a long position on a positive trend as in addition to a short position on a negative trend. In order to ensure this strategy is as effective as possible you will want to sell a low price and then buy in at an even lower point, or possibly buy in at a higher point that you know will only continue to increase.

When using this strategy it isn't as important to track patterns of reversal or continuation, all you need to do is to focus on any of the trends that may have materialized after the price break that occurred most recently. This is due to the fact that a momentum strategy is only focused on alpha returns which are only generated at the extreme sides of the spectrum. Positive momentum stocks are said to be hot as negative momentum stocks are said to be cold.

Do your research: In order to succeed with this strategy, the first thing you will want to do is to ensure you do enough research that you have a firm grasp on the state of the market. This means you will want to spend time before the market opens getting a firm grasp on the way the day is likely to play out. The stocks that have the greatest share of the public mindset are the ones that you are looking for as they are likely going to see the greatest amount of increase early on in the day. The greater the number of overall calls the stock can be expected to experience, the greater the overall likelihood that its price is going to jump or drop once the market opens for good.

Start strong: Once the market opens you will then want to keep an eye on the stocks that you earmarked as being worth watching. Depending on their performance, you will then know which direction you are going to buy into. Your goal should then be to look for prices that are increasing at rates that are higher than lower than the market as a whole, while still being in line with what you earlier research showed was expected. You should only stick with the cream of the crop when it comes to price movement in addition to total volume.

Check the charts: Once you have found the stocks that you will need to focus on for the day, you will then need to consider the current state of the charts and what they say about the position you are considering. Specifically, you will need to be on the lookout for signs that the momentum is on the rise. Once this data has been noted, it is then a simple matter of getting out ahead of it so that you will be in the position to take full advantage of it when the breakout comes to pass. In order to make money off of momentum indicators, on a reliable basis, you don't need to be the very first person to jump on a trend, you just need to jump in early enough to make money off of the latecomers. If you are at a point where you can practically watch the volume increase in real time then you have missed your window.

Finally, once all of your preparations have been made, the last thing you will need to do is wait for the right moment to move forward with your plan. Remember, just because you can determine when the breakout is most likely to occur, this doesn't mean that you can always accurately determine the total momentum you can expect. This means you are going to want to keep an eye on things throughout the time you are using this strategy to ensure it doesn't swing against you at the last moment.

Conclusion

Thank you for making it through to the end of *Stock Market Investing for Beginners:10 Great Ways to Learn Trading Psychology Revealed by a Wall Street Insider, To Reach Your Financial Freedom*, let's hope it was informative and able to provide you with all of the tools you need to achieve your goals, whatever it is that they may be. Just because you've finished this book doesn't mean there is nothing left to learn on the topic, expanding your horizons is the only way to find the mastery you seek. It is important to keep in mind that the stock market is always changing, as are the tools that other traders are using as well; if you don't commit now to becoming a lifelong learner you will eventually find that everyone else is operating on a level that you can't even begin to comprehend.

Now that you have so many new strategies to try, I know that it can be tempting to go out and try them all at once. It is important to resist this temptation, however, as doing so will only make it difficult for you to determine what worked and what didn't as all of your results will end up being mixed together. Instead, it is in your best interest to try a new strategy or two at a time and keep clear notes as to what worked and what didn't. There is no reason to expect for all of the strategies described in the previous chapters to work for you, but if even two out of the ten hit in a big way then you should have plenty of new opportunities to profit in the near future. Remember, trading in the stock market successfully is a marathon, not a sprint which means that slow and steady wins the race.

Finally, if you found this book useful in any way, a review on Amazon is always appreciated!

Description

Trading on the stock market can be an exhilarating, infuriating and, above all, profitable experience, but only if you have the strategies in place to ensure that you aren't simply throwing money at the wall and seeing what sticks. If you have a little experience trading but haven't yet found the strategies that work for you, then it can be difficult to know where to turn. Luckily, after 10 years of trading I have been through it all and have written *Stock Market Investing for Beginners: 10 Great Ways to Learn Trading Psychology Revealed by a Wall Street Insider, To Reach Your Financial Freedom* so that traders like you can learn from my mistakes.

In the following chapters, you will find strategies that focus both on fundamental and technical analysis as well as both short and long timeframes to ensure that there is something for you no matter what your trading preferences and inclinations. Give each a fair shot and you should be able to find at least a few that strike your fancy. So, what are you waiting for? Take control of your financial future and buy this book today!

Inside you will find

- Everything you need to perform a fundamental valuation
- A full breakdown of the CAN SLIM strategy
- An easy way to minimize risk to the max with the Dogs of the Dow
- Consolidation patterns to know
- ***And more...***